WHY DO WE HAVE LAWS?

By Jacqueline Laks Gorman
Reading consultant: Susan Nations, M.Ed.,
author/literacy coach/consultant in literacy development

WEEKLY READER®

PUBLISHING

Please visit our web site at www.garethstevens.com
For a free color catalog describing our list of high-quality books,
call 1-800-542-2595 (USA) or 1-800-387-3178 (Canada). Our fax: 1-877-542-2596

Library of Congress Cataloging-in-Publication Data

Gorman, Jacqueline Laks, 1955-
    Why do we have laws? / Jacqueline Laks Gorman.
        p. cm. — (Know your government)
    Includes index.
    ISBN-13: 978-0-8368-8843-0 (lib. bdg.)
    ISBN-10: 0-8368-8843-X (lib. bdg.)
    ISBN-13: 978-0-8368-8848-5 (softcover)
    ISBN-10: 0-8368-8848-0 (softcover)
    1. Law—United States—Juvenile literature. I. Title.
KF387.G66 2008
349.73—dc22   2007027916

This edition first published in 2008 by
Weekly Reader® Books
An Imprint of Gareth Stevens Publishing
1 Reader's Digest Road
Pleasantville, NY 10570-7000 USA

Copyright © 2008 by Gareth Stevens, Inc.

Senior Editor: Brian Fitzgerald
Creative Director: Lisa Donovan
Senior Designer: Keith Plechaty
Layout: Cynthia Malaran
Photo Research: Charlene Pinckney and Kimberly Babbitt

Photo credits: cover & title page Jim Arbogast/Getty Images; p. 5 Myrleen Ferguson Cate/PhotoEdit;
p. 7 © Bettmann/Corbis; p. 8 National Archives and Records Administration; p. 9 Shutterstock;
p. 11 Ron Edmonds/AP; p. 12 © Dylan Ellis/Corbis; p. 13 Jupiter Images; p. 15 Kayte Deioma/
photographersdirect.com; p. 16 © Michael Newman/PhotoEdit; p. 17 Jeff Cade/Getty Images;
p. 18 © Tim Pannell/Corbis; p. 20 © Bettmann/Corbis; p. 21 LWA-Dann Tardif/photographersdirect.com

Printed in the United States of America

1 2 3 4 5 6 7 8 9 10 09 08 07

TABLE OF CONTENTS

Words that appear in the glossary are printed in **boldface** type the first time they appear in the text.

CHAPTER 1

Following the Rules

Every day, you follow rules in school. You listen to your teacher. You do not run in the halls. You are quiet when other people talk. Think of how different your school would be if there were no rules. Classrooms would be noisy, and students would not learn as much. Some students might even get hurt.

The rules you follow in school are like the laws made by the government. Laws are rules that all people must follow. We need laws to make sure everyone is treated fairly. Laws also help keep people safe.

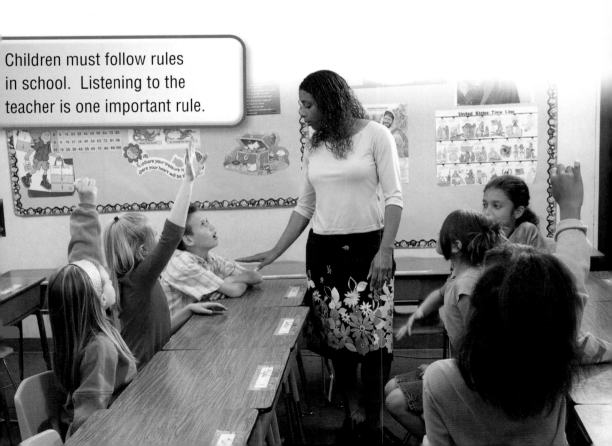

Children must follow rules in school. Listening to the teacher is one important rule.

CHAPTER 2

A Nation in Need of Laws

The area that is now the United States was once ruled by Great Britain. The British made laws that many people in America did not like. Americans wanted to write their own laws.

They decided to break away from Great Britain and form their own country. They went to war for their freedom—and they won! They called their new nation the United States.

In 1787, the leaders of the United States met to write the Constitution.

The leaders of the new nation had a hard job. They wanted to create a new government that would make fair laws. They wanted the people to have a say in what laws were created. The leaders wrote the **U.S. Constitution.** The Constitution was a plan for the new government.

We the People of the United States ...

insure domestic Tranquility, provide for the common defence, promote the gen
and our Posterity, do ordain and establish this Constitution for the United Sta

Article. I.

Section. 1. All legislative Powers herein granted shall be vested in a Congre
of Representatives.

Section. 2. The House of Representatives shall be composed of Members chosen
in each State shall have the Qualifications requi

No Person shall be a Representative
and who shall not, when elected, be an Inhabita

Representatives and direct Taxes sha

The U.S. Constitution starts with the famous words "We the People of the United States ..."

The Constitution created a government with three parts, or branches. Each branch does a different job. The **legislative branch** writes the laws for the country. This branch is called Congress. Congress is made up of the Senate and the House of Representatives.

The **executive branch** sees that the laws are carried out. The president is in charge of this branch of government.

Judges and the courts make up the **judicial branch.** The top judges sit on the Supreme Court. They decide whether laws passed in the United States are fair and follow the Constitution.

The top judges in the country meet in the Supreme Court building in Washington, D.C.

CHAPTER 3

Making Laws

Any member of Congress can propose a new law. Sometimes people suggest new laws to their **senators** and **representatives.** The president may also suggest a new law to Congress.

Members of Congress write ideas for new laws called **bills.** Senators and representatives study each bill and then vote on it.

A bill passes if most members of Congress vote for it. The bill then goes to the president. If the president signs the bill, it becomes a law. The president might not sign the bill if he or she does not agree with it. The bill can still become a law if two-thirds of both the House and Senate vote for it.

In 2003, President George W. Bush signed a bill that created a new law. The new law protected children.

States pass laws, too. Like the U.S. government, each state government has three branches. The **governor** is in charge of the state government. Each state also has a legislative branch that makes state laws. Judges in the state rule on the laws. The laws passed in each state apply only to people in the state.

State laws say that children must wear seat belts.

Cities and towns pass laws, too. The laws make the city or town a better place to live. Sometimes the people in a city or town vote on a bill before it becomes a law. State laws and city or town laws cannot disagree with national laws.

Many cities and towns have laws that tell pet owners to keep dogs on leashes.

CHAPTER 4

Enforcing Laws

The president enforces the laws passed by Congress. The president picks many people to help with this job. These men and women run government departments. They oversee education, health, and other important areas. The people in these departments see that laws are carried out.

A person who drives too fast might get a ticket. The driver will have to pay a fine.

Some people do not obey the law. People break the law when they drive too fast or do not wear seat belts. They also break the law when they steal or hurt other people. People who break the law are punished. People who break the most serious laws might be sent to jail.

Police officers work for state and local governments. Their job is to keep people safe by making sure that everyone follows the law. Police officers give tickets to people who break traffic laws. The police can also arrest people who may have committed crimes. Crimes are acts that break the law.

PARKING FOR BOOKSTORE ONLY

After a crime has been reported, the police ask questions to find out what happened.

A lot goes on in a courtroom during a trial. A judge (seated near the flag) is in charge of the court.

People who are arrested may go on **trial** in a courtroom. Parts of the Constitution protect people who are arrested. The Constitution says that the government must give everyone a fair trial. A judge makes sure the trial is fair.

A **jury** is a small group of people in the courtroom. The jury decides whether the person on trial broke the law. The judge usually decides the punishment for a guilty person. If mistakes are made during a trial, a judge may order a new trial.

The jury has an important job. Jury members must listen closely to all the facts during a trial.

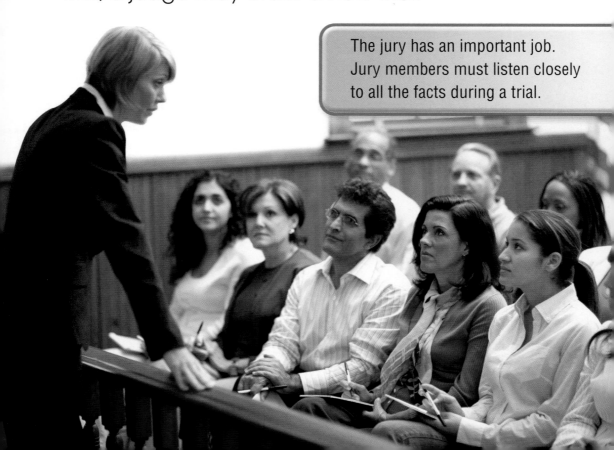

CHAPTER 5

Changing Laws

Sometimes people think that a law is unfair. They can ask Congress to change it. Years ago, African Americans in some states were not allowed to go to the same schools as white people.

Many people spoke out against these laws. Courts ruled that the laws were not fair. Congress passed new laws that said all people should be treated the same.

The Constitution can be changed, too. **Amendments** are changes to the Constitution. Amendments have brought important changes in the law. For many years, women in the United States were not allowed to vote. Women stood up for their rights. They complained to Congress. In 1920, Congress passed an amendment that gave women the right to vote.

Years ago, women did not have the right to vote. They fought for their right until the law was changed.

Some states and towns have passed laws to stop students from using cell phones in school.

The United States is always changing. As the country changes, new problems arise. The law is always changing to solve these problems and to protect our way of life.

Glossary

amendment: an official change made to the U.S. Constitution

bill: a written plan for a new law

executive branch: the part of a government that enforces the laws

governor: the head of a state government

judicial branch: the part of a government that decides whether laws are fair

jury: a small group of people who decide during a trial whether someone has broken the law

legislative branch: the part of a government that makes the laws

representative: a member of the House of Representatives, one of the two parts of Congress

senator: a member of the Senate, one of the two parts of Congress

trial: the official process of deciding in a court of law whether someone did something wrong

U.S. Constitution: a document that states how the United States is governed

To Find Out More

Books
Government: How Local, State, and Federal Government Works.
Our Government and Citizenship (series).
Mark Friedman (Child's World)

Making Laws: A Look at How a Bill Becomes a Law. How Government
Works (series). Sandy Donovan (Lerner Publishing Group)

The U.S. Constitution and You. Sy Sobel (Barron's Educational Series)

Web Sites
What Is a Law?
bensguide.gpo.gov/3-5/lawmaking/index.html
Learn what laws are and how they are made in the United States.

How Laws Are Made
clerkkids.house.gov/laws/index.html
This House of Representatives site for kids lets readers follow a bill
on its way to becoming a law.

Publisher's note to educators and parents: Our editors have carefully reviewed
these web sites to ensure that they are suitable for children. Many web sites
change frequently, however, and we cannot guarantee that a site's future
contents will continue to meet our high standards of quality and educational
value. Be advised that children should be closely supervised whenever they
access the Internet.

Index

About the Author

Jacqueline Laks Gorman grew up in New York City. She attended Barnard College and Columbia University, where she received a master's degree in American history. She has worked on many kinds of books and has written several series for children and young adults. She now lives in DeKalb, Illinois, with her husband, David, and children, Colin and Caitlin. She registered to vote when she turned eighteen and votes in every election.